THE ANIMAL KINGDOM

Fish

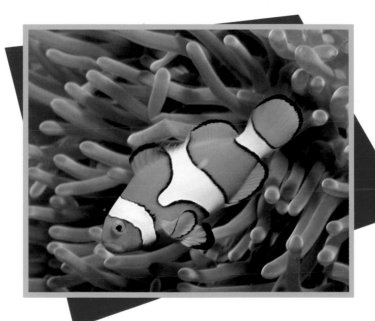

Bev Harvey

CHELSEA CLUBHOUSE

An Imprint of Chelsea House Publishers
A Haights Cross Communications Company
Philadelphia

This edition first published in 2003 in the United States of America by Chelsea Clubhouse, a division of Chelsea House Publishers and a subsidiary of Haights Cross Communications.

Chelsea Clubhouse
1974 Sproul Road, Suite 400
Broomall, PA 19008-0914

The Chelsea House world wide web address is www.chelseahouse.com

Library of Congress Cataloging-in-Publication Data

Harvey, Bev.
    Fish / by Bev Harvey.
    p. cm. — (The animal kingdom)
    Summary: A simple introduction to the characteristics of fish in general and of select species.
    ISBN 0-7910-6982-6
    1. Fishes—Juvenile literature. [1. Fishes.] I. Title.
    QL617.2 .H37 2003
    597—dc21

                                                            2002000978

First published in 2002 by
MACMILLAN EDUCATION AUSTRALIA PTY LTD
627 Chapel Street, South Yarra, Australia, 3141

Copyright © Bev Harvey 2002
Copyright in photographs © individual photographers as credited

Edited by Angelique Campbell-Muir
Page layout by Domenic Lauricella

Printed in China

Acknowledgements

Cover photograph: Clownfish, courtesy of Kevin Deacon/Auscape.

Fred Adler, p. 16; Kelvin Aitken, pp. 12 (all), 25, 26, 27, 28; ANT Photo Library, pp. 6 (all), 7 (center), 10, 13, 24; Bill & Peter Boyle/Auscape, p. 14; Dr Heinz Gert de Couet/Auscape, p. 8; Kevin Deacon/Auscape, pp. 1, 7 (bottom); Jeff Foott/Auscape, pp. 21, 22; Labat-Lanceau/Auscape, pp. 4, 18; D. Parer & E. Parer-Cook/Auscape, p. 20; Doug Perrine/Auscape, p. 15; Mark Spencer/Auscape, p. 9; Yvette Tavernier-Bios/Auscape, p. 17; Mark Webster—Oxford Scientific Films/Auscape, p. 5; Australian Picture Library/Corbis, pp. 7 (top), 23; Getty Images, p. 29; Geoff Taylor/Lochman Transparencies, p. 11; Dave Thompson, p. 19.

While every care has been taken to trace and acknowledge copyright, the publisher tenders their apologies for any accidental infringement where copyright has proved untraceable.

Contents

Fish

Fish are vertebrates. A vertebrate is an animal that has a backbone. Fish need water to survive. They have **gills** so they can breathe underwater.

Nearly all fish have fins to help them move in water. Many fish have scales that cover their bodies. Fish are **cold-blooded** animals.

Most fish live in the salt water of seas and oceans. They can be found in warm, tropical waters as well as in freezing cold waters near the poles. Other fish live in freshwater streams, rivers, ponds, and lakes.

Types of Fish

There are many types of fish.

White sharks live in cool areas of oceans. They hunt in coastal waters.

Lampreys live in freshwater streams and in the sea.

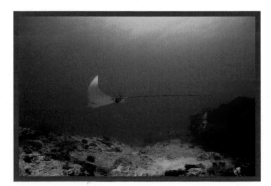

Stingrays live in warm, shallow seawater.

Electric eels live in muddy rivers in South America. They can shock their **prey** with electricity.

Most trout live in freshwater streams and lakes.

Clownfish live in tropical areas of oceans.

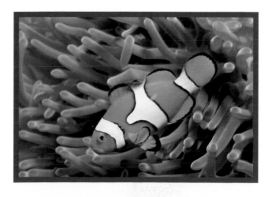

Features of Fish

Skeleton

Most fish have skeletons made of bone. Tuna, trout, and goldfish all have bony skeletons. Most bony fish also have bones in their fins. Sharks and rays have skeletons made of cartilage. Cartilage is strong tissue that is more flexible than bone.

Movement

Fish have a smooth, streamlined shape. They move easily through the water. To swim, they sweep their tail fins and move their bodies from side to side. Fish use their other fins to balance, steer, and slow down.

Appearance

Fish can be many shapes and colors. Sharks are large and powerful. Lampreys are long and thin. Rays are wide but flat. Some fish have dull colors to help them blend into rocks or sand. Others are brightly colored.

Breathing

Fish breathe. A fish gulps water into its mouth. The water filters through its gills. The gills remove oxygen from the water. The oxygen passes into the fish's bloodstream.

gills

Eating Habits

Most fish are carnivores. Carnivores eat meat. Carnivorous fish eat worms, shellfish, water animals, and even other fish. Some fish are herbivores. Herbivores eat plants.

Carnivorous fish eat meat, such as other fish.

Herbivorous fish eat plants.

Most fish have jaws and teeth. They can bite and tear their food into pieces. Lampreys do not have jaws. They suck food into their mouths.

Barracudas use their sharp teeth to catch and eat other fish.

Young Fish

Most female fish lay eggs, and then male fish **fertilize** the eggs. Many of the fertilized eggs hatch. But not all young fish survive. Some are eaten by other animals.

Some fish give birth to live young.
The female's eggs hatch inside her body.
The young look like small adults when
they are born.

Pet Goldfish

Goldfish are freshwater fish. They originally came from China. They have large eyes and a good sense of smell. Some people keep goldfish as pets. Pet goldfish live in aquariums and garden ponds.

Goldfish are omnivorous. This means they eat both meat and plants. Pet goldfish eat pellets and dried flakes, which are sold in pet shops. Goldfish in the wild eat tiny plants and animals found on the pond floor.

17

Pet goldfish can **breed** all year round if they live in a warm aquarium. In the wild, goldfish breed only in summer, when it is warm.

Goldfish eggs

A female goldfish lays up to 1,000 eggs at a time, but some of them will not hatch. A male fertilizes them. The eggs take about four days to hatch.

Pacific Salmon

Adult Pacific salmon live in the Pacific Ocean. But they were born in freshwater lakes and streams. Many types of salmon return to the place of their birth to spawn, or reproduce.

Adult Pacific salmon live in the ocean for up to seven years. They eat shrimp, squid, and small fish. When they are ready to spawn, the salmon swim up freshwater rivers.

Some salmon swim as far as 2,000 miles (3,200 kilometers) from the ocean. They stop eating. They live off their body fat.

The female salmon digs and lays eggs in several nests. A male fertilizes each nest of eggs. After they spawn, the adults die. The eggs hatch in two to four months.

White Sharks

White sharks live in the ocean. They hunt along coastlines, but they are also found in deep waters. They live on their own.

Female white sharks do not lay eggs. They give birth to live young, called pups. They have litters of two to ten pups at a time. Female sharks do not give birth every year.

25

White sharks hunt for their food. They bite their prey and wait until the prey is weak from its injuries. Then the shark kills the prey and eats it.

White sharks eat tuna and other fish, sea birds, sea turtles, and seals. The number of white sharks in the world is dropping. Some countries have laws to protect white sharks.

Endangered Common Sturgeon

The common sturgeon is an **endangered** fish that is found only in Europe. They live in the ocean, but they return to freshwater streams to lay their eggs. Humans catch sturgeon for their meat and their eggs. People use the eggs to make a food called caviar.

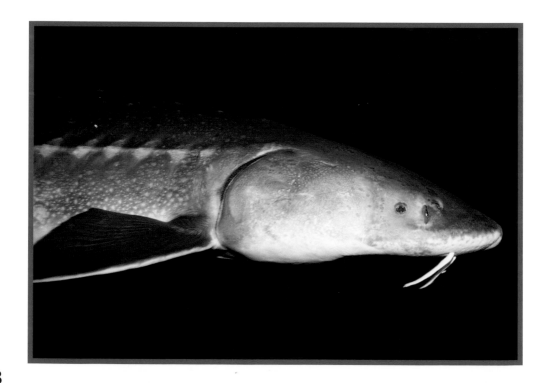

Caviar is eaten by people around the world.

Some streams have dams across them that stop the sturgeon from going upstream to lay eggs. People are helping to save the common sturgeon by raising and releasing young sturgeon back into the wild.

Animal Classification

The animal kingdom is divided into two main groups of animals: invertebrates and vertebrates. In this book, you have read about fish.

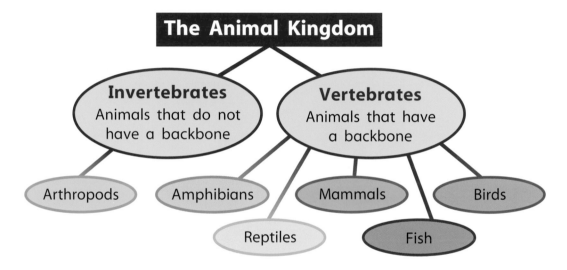

Question What have you learned about fish?

Answer Fish are:
- vertebrates
- cold-blooded
- able to swim
- able to breathe underwater.

Glossary

breed   to come together to create young

cold-blooded   an animal whose body temperature changes to match the temperature of the air, ground, or water around it

endangered   a type of animal or plant that may soon die out

fertilize   to join male and female cells in order to produce young

gill   part of an animal's body that allows it to take in oxygen from water

prey   an animal hunted for food

Index